Broth Recip

Delicious Broth Recipes for The Amateur Cook!

BY: Valeria Ray

License Notes

• • • • • • • • • ● ● ● ● ● ● • • • • ••

Table of Contents

Introduction

Bone broth has been around for decades, with generations of chefs and cooks touting the amazing health benefits of consuming broth on a regular basis. Packed with nutrients and minerals, broth is heralded by some as the "elixir of life" Ready to start your own journey? Read on to discover 30 delicious broth and stock recipes and how to use them!

1. Chicken bone broth

Clear and delicate, this broth is nice sipped on its own or used as a base for soups dotted with vegetables and fortified by grains or starchy potatoes.

Makes: 4 quarts

Time: 8 to 18 hours

Ingredients:

- The spent frame of 1 roasted chicken
- ½ cup dry white wine
- 4–6 quarts cold water

Instructions:

Place the bones into a heavy stock-pot, add in wine, and add cold water. Make sure to immerse the chicken feet by 1 inch (about 5 quarts). Cover pot and boil over med-high heat. Then lower heat to med-low.

Covered, let it simmer for at least 8 and up to 18 hours or until rich and fragrant, and the bones crumble on touch. Skim off foam that appears on the surface of the broth and discard it.

Strain the broth through a fine-mesh sieve. Use the stock right away or transfer into four 1-quart sized jars, sealing their lids tightly. Chill up to 7 days or freeze for 6 months.

2. Roasted turkey bone broth

This broth calls for turkey's bones mixed with aromatic vegetables, bay leaves, and black pepper to make a rich, golden-colored bone broth.

Makes: 4 quarts

Time: 14 to 24 hours

Ingredients:

- Bones of 1 roasted turkey
- 4 carrots, chopped roughly
- 6 celery stalks, chopped roughly
- 1 large yellow onion, unpeeled, quartered
- 2 bay leaves
- 1 tbsp. Whole black peppercorns
- ½ cup dry white wine
- 5 quarts cold water

Instructions:

Place the bones into a heavy stock-pot, add in the veggies and spices. Add wine and cold water. Cover pot and boil over med-high heat. Then lower heat to med-low.

Covered, let it simmer for at least 14 and up to 24 hours or until rich and fragrant, and the bones crumble on touch. Skim off foam that appears on the surface of the broth and discard it.

Strain the broth through a fine-mesh sieve. Use the stock right away or transfer into four 1-quart sized jars, sealing their lids tightly. Chill up to 7 days or freeze for 6 months.

3. Simmered roasted beef bone broth

A combination of fatty marrowbones, meaty neck bones and joints work very well to create a broth which is at once luxuriant, flavorsome and silky in texture

Makes: 4 quarts

Time: 12 to 18 hours

Ingredients:

- 5 pounds beef soup bones
- 1 cup red wine
- 4–6 quarts cold water

Instructions:

Preheat oven to 425°f.

In a single layer, roast bones for 45 minutes.

Place the bones into a heavy stock-pot. Add wine and cold water. Cover pot and boil over med-high heat. Then lower heat to med-low.

Covered, let it simmer for at least 12 and up to 18 hours, adding water if necessary to keep bones submerged.

Strain the broth through a fine-mesh sieve. Use the stock right away or transfer into four 1-quart sized jars, sealing their lids tightly. Chill up to 7 days or freeze for 6 months. Be sure to remove hardened fat off the top. You can use this to cook with or discard it.

4. Fish stock

Fish bones don't need as much coaxing to release their nutrients as beef bones do, and so just a short while in the pot, less than an hour, is sufficient to give you a good, nutritive fish stock.

Makes: 4-6 quarts

Time: 25 minutes

Ingredients:

- 5 lb. Fish trimmings
- 8 oz. Dry white wine
- 4–6 quarts cold water

Instructions:

Place the trimmings into a heavy stock-pot. Add wine and cold water. Cover pot and bring to bare simmer over med heat. Skim off any foam that may arise.

Let it simmer for about 25 minutes.

Strain broth through a fine sieve. Use the stock right away or transfer into 4, 1-quart sized jars, sealing their lids. Store up to 5 days or freeze for 6 months.

5. Dashi

Dashi is a clear, mild and smoky broth with hints of fish.

Makes: about 3 cups

Time: 15 to 20 minutes

Ingredients:

- 4 cups cold water
- 1 (6-inch) strip kombu
- 1 cup bonito flakes

Instructions:

To a saucepan, add kombu and water.

Cover pot and bring to bare simmer over med heat. Remove kombu and discard.

Add in the flakes and turn off heat. Allow to sit for about 10 minutes.

Strain broth through a fine sieve. Use the stock right away or transfer into 4, 1-quart sized jars, sealing their lids. Store up to 5 days or freeze for 6 months.

6. Chicken foot broth

Chicken feet generally get a bad rep for being rather unsighlty. But once you get past their visual appeal, you'll reap the rewards in a delicious flavor-rich broth!

Makes about 4 quarts

Time: 8 to 12 hours

Ingredients:

- 3 pounds prepared chicken feet
- ¼ cup white wine
- 5 quarts cold water

Instructions:

Place the chicken feet into a heavy stock-pot, add in wine, and add cold water. Make sure to immerse the chicken feet by 1 inch (about 5 quarts). Cover pot and boil over med-high heat. Then lower to med-low.

Uncovered, let it simmer for 8 and up to 12 hours. Add water to keep the feet submerged. Skim off foam that appears on the surface of the broth and discard it.

Strainusing a fine-mesh sieve. Discard the spent feet, as you won't need them after you've made the stock.

Use the stock right away or transfer into four 1-quart sized jars, sealing lids tightly.

A thin layer of yellow fat may rise to the surface of your refrigerated or frozen stock and harden; spoon off and discard the fat before cooking with the stock.

7. Shellfish stock

Shellfish shells are rich in trace minerals making them a very healthy option to consider while making broth

Makes: about 2 quarts

Time: 60 to 65 minutes

Ingredients:

- 1 pound shellfish shells
- 1 cup dry white wine
- 2–4 quarts cold water

Instructions:

Preheat oven to 400°f.

In a single layer, roast shells for 20 minutes.

Place the bones into a heavy stock-pot. Add wine and cold water. Cover pot and boil over med-high heat. Then lower heat to med-low. Skim off any foam that may arise.

Let it simmer for at about 45 minutes or until fragrant.

Strain the broth through a fine-mesh sieve. Use the stock right away or transfer into four 1-quart sized jars, sealing their lids tightly. Chill up to 7 days or freeze for 6 months. Be sure to remove hardened fat off the top. You can use this to cook with or discard it.

8. Kitchen scrap broth

This recipe utilizes leftover kitchen scraps to make a delicious broth!

Makes: about 4 quarts

Time: 8 to 12 hours

Ingredients:

- 2 to 3 pounds leftover chicken bones or chicken scraps like necks, backs, and wings
- 2½ cups loosely packed vegetable trimmings, such as onion skins, carrot peelings, celery leaves, and parsley stems
- 2 dried bay leaves
- 1 tablespoon whole black peppercorns
- 2 tablespoons white wine vinegar
- 4–6 quarts cold water

Instructions:

Dump all of the ingredients into a heavy stockpot and then pour enough water into the pot to cover by 1 inch (about 4–6 quarts). Cover pot and boil over med-high heat. Then lower heat to med-low.

Covered, let it simmer for at least 8 and up to 12 hours, adding water if necessary to keep bones submerged.

Strain broth through a fine sieve. Use the stock right away or transfer into 4, 1-quart sized jars, sealing their lids. Store up to 5 days or freeze for 6 months.

9. Green broth

Adding vegetables, particularly leafy greens, to broth infuses it with not only bright vegetal notes but also minerals!

Makes about 2 quarts, ready in 20 to 25 minutes

Ingredients

- 1 bunch parsley, coarsely chopped
- 1 bunch kale, coarsely chopped
- 1 bunch watercress, coarsely chopped
- 3 celery stalks, coarsely chopped
- 4 green onions, coarsely chopped
- 6 cloves garlic, coarsely chopped
- 1 (6-inch) strip kombu
- 2–3 quarts cold water or whole chicken broth

Instructions:

Add all ingredients to a pot. Bring to a bare simmer on med-high heat. Continue cooking, covered, for 20 minutes.

Strain broth through a fine sieve. Use the stock right away or transfer into 4, 1-quart sized jars, sealing their lids. Store up to 5 days or freeze for 6 months.

10. Mushroom broth

Roasting the mushrooms creates a strong flavor - enhancing the savory and meaty base notes!

Makes about 2 quarts

Time: 1 hour

Ingredients:

- ¾ lb. Mixed mushrooms, chopped into ½-inch pieces
- 2 small yellow onions, cut in half
- 3 cloves garlic, crushed
- 1 tbsp. Olive oil
- 2 quarts cold water or chicken broth
- ¼ cup dry white wine
- 6 sprigs thyme

Instructions:

Preheat the oven to 425°f.

Arrange mushrooms on a baking sheet. Squeeze in onion halves into the mushrooms, and top with the garlic. Sprinkle with the oil and roast for 20 minutes.

Once roasted, move to a pot. Add the rest of the ingredients and bring it all to a simmer over med-high heat. Continue simmering, covered, for about 30 minutes.

Strain broth through a fine sieve. Use the stock right away or transfer into 2, 1-quart sized jars, sealing their lids. Store up to 5 days or freeze for 6 months.

11. Sea vegetable broth

Sea vegetables are extraordinarily rich in minerals, particularly iodine, which helps support thyroid health. You can find dried seaweed available for purchase in many natural foods stores.

Makes about 2 quarts,

Time: 25 to 30 minutes

Ingredients:

- 6 green onions, chopped into 1-inch pieces
- 2 celery stalks, chopped into 1-inch pieces
- 1 carrot, chopped into 1-inch pieces
- 1 (6-inch) strip kombu
- 1 leaf dried dulse
- 8 dried shiitakes
- 2–3 quarts cold water

Instructions:

Add all ingredients to a pot. Bring to a bare simmer on med-high heat. Continue cooking, covered, for 20 minutes.

Strain broth through a fine sieve. Use the stock right away or transfer into 2, 1-quart sized jars, sealing their lids. Store up to 5 days or freeze for 6 months.

12. Remouillage

Remouillage is weaker in flavor than a stock made with bones used for the first time, but you'll still extract some flavor, some protein, and trace minerals a second time, too, helping you waste even less in the kitchen.

Makes about 2 quarts,

Time: 6 to 8 hours

Ingredients:

- The spent bones from a batch of stock or bone broth
- ½ cup red or white wine, or as needed
- 2–3 quarts cold water

Instructions:

Place the bones into a heavy stock-pot, add in wine, and add cold water. Make sure to immerse the chicken feet by 1 inch (about 5 quarts). Cover pot and boil over med-high heat. Then lower heat to med-low. Cook for 8 hours.

Strain broth through a fine sieve. Use the stock right away or transfer into 2, 1-quart sized jars, sealing their lids. Store up to 5 days or freeze for 6 months.

13. Thai vegetable broth

This broth is sumptuously spiced and seasoned without being overly spicy. Despite being a meat dish, the broth is quite light but heavy on flavor!

Total Time: 40m

Servings: 4-6

Ingredients:

- Paste
- 1 tbsp. Oil
- 1 tsp cilantro seeds
- 1 tsp cumin powder
- 4 cardamom pods
- 8 cloves
- Pinch of fennel seeds
- 6 red shallots, chopped
- 3 garlic cloves, chopped
- 1 tsp lemongrass, finely chopped
- 1 tsp galangal, finely chopped
- 4 dried red chilies
- 1 tsp nutmeg powder
- 1 tsp white pepper powder
- 1 tbsp. Oil
- 1 cup chopped baby onions
- 1 lb. Potatoes
- 10½ oz. Baby carrots, cut into 1¼ inch pieces
- 8 oz. Button mushrooms
- 1 cinnamon sprig
- A bay leaf
- 1 tin coconut cream

- 3 tsp palm sugar
- 1 tbsp. Lime juice
- 1 tbsp. Thai basil, finely chopped
- 1 tbsp. Roasted peanuts

Instructions:

Heat oil in pan over. Add coriander, cumin, cloves, fennel and cardamom. Cook for a couple of minutes.

To a food processor, add the paste ingredients along with the spices. Process till smooth.

Heat oil in a pan, add spice paste. Cook for 2 minutes.

Add the veggies, cinnamon sprig, leaf and about 2 cups water. Bring mixture to a boil.

Reduce heat and simmer, keeping the mixture covered, for half an hour. Vegetables should be cooked.

Fold through the cream and cook, for a few minutes, until thick.

Sprinkle in the lime juice, sugar and basil. Serve topped with peanuts!

14. Roasted garlic beef stock

The toasting of the garlic enhances the flavor of this delicious beef stock!

Serves: 10

Time: 45m

Ingredients:

- 4 lb. Beef bones
- 1/2 bunch coarsely chopped celery
- 1 coarsely chopped medium onion
- 4 chopped medium carrots
- 1 tbsp. Tomato paste
- 1/2 cup olive oil
- 1 head of garlic, sliced
- 1 bunch herb stems
- 4 bay leaves
- 1/2 tsp black peppercorns
- 1/2 tsp coriander seeds

Directions:

Preheat oven to 450°f. On a lined sheet, roast the bones for about half an hour. Place the carrots, onion, and celery over the sheet, and roast further for about 10 minutes. Pour and spread the tomato paste over the vegetables and bones, and roast further for about 5 minutes. Let it sit and cool.

In the meantime, sauté the garlic in oil for until golden in a small saucepan placed over medium heat. Using a fine-mesh sieve, strain the oil into a bowl for other uses, and set aside the garlic.

Transfer roasted ingredients s to a large stockpot placed over medium heat. Pour in cold water to cover. Add in the reserved garlic, coriander seeds, peppercorns, bay leaves, and herb stems. Bring to a boil. Turn the heat low, and allow simmering for about 3 hours, skimming foam and fat from surface. Through a fine-mesh sieve, strain the stock into a large bowl. Discard the solids after pressing for all their juices.

15. Beef bone stock with tomato

Delicious, and tart, this is a great base for a tomato soup!

Serves: 8

Time: 24 – 30 hours

Ingredients:

- 1 (6 ounce) can tomato paste
- 2 pounds beef bones
- 6 cups cool water, or as needed
- 2 onions, thickly sliced
- 2 carrots
- 3 cloves garlic, crushed
- 2 bay leaves

Instructions:

Preheat oven to 400 degrees f.

Rub tomato paste onto the surfaces of the beef bones and place them on to a lightly greased roasting pan.

Bake for about 30 minutes until the bones start to brown.

Once roasted, transfer them to a pot. Pour in water, just enough to cover the bones. Add in the bay leaves, carrots, and onions.

Cook the broth over low heat for 24 - 30 hours.

Through a fine mesh sieve, strain the broth into a container. Store the broth by chilling.

16. Slow cooker chicken broth

This slow cooker chicken broth recipes makes for the easiest stock!

Serves: 5

Time: 10 hours 15 minutes

Ingredients:

- 2 1/2 pounds bone-in chicken bits
- 6 cups water
- 2 stalks celery, cut into small pieces
- 2 carrots, roughly chopped
- 1 onion, quartered
- 1 tablespoon dried basil

Directions:

In a slow cooker, place the basil, onion, celery, water and the chicken pieces.

Cook on low setting for about 10 hours. Through a fine mesh sieve, strain the broth into a container. Discard any strained solids. Store the broth by chilling.

17. Scotch broth

Delicious, and filling, this scotch broth recipe is a guaranteed crowd please!

Serves: 8

Time: 3 hours

Ingredients:

- 2 pounds beef shank soup bones
- 2 quarts water
- 6 black peppercorns, whole
- 1 cup chopped carrots
- 1 cup turnips, chopped
- 1 cup chopped celery
- 1/2 cup chopped onion
- 1/4 cup pearl barley

Directions:

Combine the peppercorns, water, and soup bones in a large stockpot. Bring to a boil. Cover, and allow simmering for about 90 minutes until the meat easily comes off the bones.

Take out the bones and strain the broth. Allow chilling.

Skim the fat off. Take out the meat from bones, and dice. Return the diced meat in the broth, including the barley, onion, celery, turnips, and carrots. Bring to a boil. Turn the heat low, cover and allow simmering for about an hour until the barley and vegetables are tender.

18. Asian chicken broth

This light, lively broth features shiitake mushrooms, lemongrass, garlic, and cilantro and is absolutely delicious!

Time: 15 minutes

Yield: 4 cups

Ingredients:

- 4 cups chicken broth
- 1 length lemongrass, cut into 1-inch pieces
- 1 clove garlic, crushed
- Handful of shiitake mushrooms, diced
- 2 green onions, cut into ½-inch pieces
- Himalayan salt
- Black pepper
- 2 tbsp. coarsely chopped cilantro leaves

Instructions:

In a saucepan, heat the broth on med heat. All veggies. Reduce heat to med-low or low for a bare simmer. Cook for 5 to 10 minutes.

Discard the lemongrass and garlic. Season and top with the cilantro.

19. Eastern European beef bone broth

Shredded cabbage and dill give this broth an old world twist. The cabbage helps to fill you up without adding carbs.

Makes: 1 quart

Time: 20m

Ingredients:

- 4 cups beef broth
- 1 clove garlic, crushed
- 1/2 cup cabbage, shredded
- 1 chopped rib celery
- 1 bay leaf
- 1 tsp dill
- 1 black peppercorn
- Himalayan salt

Instructions:

In a pot, heat the broth on med heat. Add all ingredients except salt.

Reduce heat to med-low or low for a bare simmer. Cook just until the veggies are tender - about 5 to 10 minutes.

Discard spices. Season with salt and serve.

20. French onion beef bone broth

This broth's secret to success: the onions cook low and slow until they caramelize, giving them a rich, sweet flavor.

Makes: 1 quart

Time: 20m

Ingredients:

- 4 cups beef bone broth
- 1 clove garlic, crushed
- 1 cup roasted sweet onions
- ¼ tsp. Herbes de provence
- 1 black peppercorn
- Himalayan salt

Instructions:

In a saucepan, heat the broth over medium heat. Add the garlic, onions, herbs, and peppercorn. Reduce heat to med-low or low for bare simmer. Cook for 5 to 10 minutes.

Remove and discard the spices. Season with salt and serve.

21. Italian beef bone broth

Basil, garlic, and tomato sauce make this broth delizioso .

I like serving it as an appetizer when I have company for dinner.

Makes: 1 quart

Time: 20m

Ingredients:

- 4 cups beef bone broth
- 1 clove garlic, crushed
- ¼ cup no-sugar-added tomato sauce
- ¼ tsp. Italian seasoning
- Himalayan salt
- Freshly ground black pepper
- 6 fresh basil leaves, cut into a fine chiffonade

Instructions:

In a saucepan, heat the broth on med heat. Add garlic, tomato sauce, and Italian seasoning. Reduce heat to med-low or low for a bare simmer. Cook for 5 to 10 minutes.

Season and serve topped with basil.

22. Thanksgiving Turkey Broth

I call this broth "Thanksgiving in a mug." And you know what? I think I like it better than the turkey dinner!

Makes: 4 cups

Time: 20 minutes

Ingredients:

- 4 cups (1 quart) Turkey Bone Broth
- 2 ribs celery, finely chopped
- 1 carrot, finely chopped
- 1 small clove garlic, smashed
- ¼–½ teaspoon ground sage
- 1 whole clove
- Celtic or pink Himalayan salt
- Freshly ground black pepper

Instructions:

In a saucepan, heat the broth over medium heat. Add the celery, carrot, garlic, sage, and clove. Reduce heat to med-low or low for a bare simmer. Cook just until the carrots and celery are tender, 5 to 10 minutes.

Remove and discard the garlic and clove. Season with salt and pepper and serve.

23. Oxtail Meat Stock and Bone Broth

This makes a neutral, gelatin-rich bone broth that is very easy and uses bones that tend to be more available in grocery or health-food stores.

Total **Time:** 4–25 hours

Yield: 3–4 quarts

Ingredients:

- 1 (7") marrowbone —use several marrowbones totaling up to 7" if you have smaller pieces
- 3–4 lbs. oxtail bones
- 1 split pig's foot
- ¼ cup apple cider vinegar

Instructions:

Preheat oven to 350° F.

Put the marrowbones with the split middles facing up (if you have split marrowbones; otherwise, just put the smaller pieces or whole marrowbone in flat), oxtails, and pig's foot into a deep baking dish (to catch the melted fat).

Roast the marrowbones, oxtails, and pig's foot in the oven for about 30–40 minutes or until the oxtail meat is darker brown. If you like, turn the oxtail bones and pig's foot over at the 15-minute mark (optional).

Once the bones are roasted, remove the marrow from the marrowbones.

Add them to your chosen pot and add enough water to just cover the bones and meat. Then add the apple cider vinegar.

Let the bones, water, and apple cider vinegar sit for an hour before turning on the burner. After an hour, put the burner on medium high, bring to a boil, and then reduce the heat to the lowest temperature to simmer. Simmer for as long as you like (up to 3 hours for stock, and up to 24 hours for richer broth).

Once the stock or broth is finished simmering, allow it to cool down. Then get a large bowl and a fine mesh strainer to strain the broth. With a cup, jar, or ladle, pour broth through the strainer, saving the liquid in your large bowl and straining out the bones. Set the strainer with bones aside for a moment.

24. Rocket Stock

This is the bone broth version of "Bulletproof Coffee," and is in fact better for you!

Makes: 1-2 servings

Time: 5 minutes

Ingredients:

- 1–2 cups bone broth of choice, warmed
- Sea salt, to taste
- 1 Tbsp. butter or ghee
- 1 Tbsp. coconut oil

Instructions:

Combine ingredients in a blender.

Blend on high for 1–2 minutes.

Enjoy!

25. Healing Chicken Soup

This recipe is a healing potion that makes its own chicken bone broth!

Makes: 8-10 servings

Total Time: 6½ hours

Ingredients:

- Whole chicken cut into parts
- 6 slices fresh astragalus root
- 7 codonopsis roots
- 1 Tbsp. dried, ground dioscorea
- ¼ tsp. ground schizandra berries
- 2 Tbsp. whole goji berries, ground
- 2 tsp. dried ground ophiopogon
- 1 (2") piece of kombu
- ¼ cup dried wakame
- 2 tsp. coriander powder
- 1 fresh pear, chopped
- 2 tsp. sea salt
- Black pepper, to taste

Instructions:

Put chicken in a large pot or slow cooker. Cover chicken with water.

On high, bring liquid to a boil, then reduce to a slow simmer. Cook for 4–6 hours.

Add in remaining ingredients, except the coriander and fresh pear.

Add coriander and fresh pear in the last 45 minutes of cooking

Season and serve!

26. Dong Quai Chicken Soup

Dong quai and astragalus are adaptogenic herbs that protect the body from stress. This combination is especially good for someone experiencing anemia, chronic fatigue, hormone imbalance, or any conditions of weakness.

Makes: 8-10 servings

Time: 6 ½h

Ingredients:

- Whole chicken cut into parts
- 1 Tbsp. dried dong quai root; avoid using this herb if you are pregnant, have diarrhea, or have digestive pain.
- 1 Tbsp. dried astragalus (or 6 slices fresh astragalus)
- 1 cup fresh or 2 Tbsp. dried shiitake mushrooms
- Sea salt and black pepper, to taste
- Optional: Honey, to taste
- Toasted sesame oil, to taste
- Green onion, sliced thin, to taste

Instructions:

Put chicken in a large pot or slow cooker. Cover chicken with water.

Add the dong quai, astragalus, and shiitake mushrooms.

Setting your burner to high, bring the liquid to a boil, then reduce to a slow simmer. Simmer for 4–6 hours.

Add sea salt and pepper. You can also sweeten this soup with a bit of honey, if desired, to balance the taste of the medicinal herbs.

27. Joint Health Broth

Makes: 1 serving

Time: 8-12h

Ingredients:

- 1⅓ cup chicken bone broth or stock (you can also use the Healing Elixir Vegetable Stock)
- 1 Tbsp. crushed dried bay leaves

Instructions:

Place both ingredients into a pot. Simmer for 5 minutes.

Allow to steep overnight in a thermos.

Strain out and discard the bay leaves.

Sip liquid this in small amounts throughout the day.

28. Egg Broth Soup

Poached, scrambled, or hard-boiled, people love eggs in soup! Try this delicious healing recipe for rainy days at home.

Makes: 2 servings

Time: 10m

Ingredients:

- 1½ cups bone broth
- Choice of spices
- 4–6 eggs
- 1 Tbsp. crushed dried bay leaves

Instructions:

Warm up broth with your choice of additions.

Simmer on medium high for a few minutes.

Mix the eggs in for a few minutes.

You soup is ready when the egg turns opaque!

29. Hearty Hamburger Soup

This recipe makes a hearty, tasty meal that cooks up in minutes for a fast breakfast, lunch, or dinner.

Makes: 2-4 servings

Time: 10m

Ingredients:

- 2 Tbsp. coconut oil, ghee, or butter
- 2 tsp. turmeric
- 2 tsp. black pepper
- 3 cups bone broth, meat stock, or the Healing Elixir Vegetable stock (you could also use 2 cups broth or stock and 1 cup water)
- ½ lb. ground beef (this also works with ground bison, lamb, turkey, or chicken)
- 2 tsp. sea salt
- Optional: 1 cup thinly shredded bok choy or thinly sliced yellow summer squash and zucchini

Instructions:

Add coconut oil, ghee, or butter to a saucepan and set your burner to low.

Add the rest of the spices, except for the sea salt. Warm the spices in the coconut oil for 2 minutes or until you can smell their aromas.

Add the bone broth or stock and sea salt. Simmer for 1 minute.

Add the ground beef in small chunks. Decide if you want any sliced vegetables, like bok choy and yellow summer squash. Add them if you want them. Simmer the broth with meat (and vegetables, if using) for 3 minutes or until the meat has changed color and looks done. Ground meat, bok choy, and yellow squash cook very fast in broth.

Taste the broth and, if you want, you can dilute it with more water.

Add more sea salt and pepper, if needed.

30. Healing Asparagus Soup

This recipe can use any meat or poultry bone broth. Not only is it delicious; it's very healing, too!

Makes: 4 cups

Time: 10m

Ingredients:

- 2 Tbsp. butter, ghee, or coconut oil
- 1 tsp. black pepper
- 2 tsp. turmeric
- ½ tsp. ground cumin seed
- 1 clove garlic, minced
- 3 cups broth or stock
- 2 cups asparagus, chopped
- 1 tsp. sea salt

Instructions:

Add the butter to a 3-quart saucepan and set the burner to low. Melt the butter and add the black pepper, turmeric, and ground cumin. Heat for 2 minutes on low, to release the aromas and medicinal properties of the spices. Add the minced garlic and heat for 2 more minutes.

Add the broth and raise the heat to high, bringing the broth to a boil. Once the broth is boiling, add the asparagus and reduce the heat, bringing the water to a simmer. Simmer for 5 minutes.

Now add the sea salt and puree the soup. Use a handheld immersion blender or a potato masher to mash up the asparagus, blending it with the broth. Blend until smooth.

Pour into bowls and serve. Add sea salt, pepper, butter, sesame oil, or bite-size pieces of avocado to each bowl, to taste.

Conclusion

And there you have it! 30 delicious and super healthy broth and stock recipes! Which one are you most excited to try? We hope this has been useful and left you feeling inspired to lead you on a healthier, more fulfilling path towards delicious, clean food!

About the Author

A native of Indianapolis, Indiana, Valeria Ray found her passion for cooking while she was studying English Literature at Oakland City University. She decided to try a cooking course with her friends and the experience changed her forever. She enrolled at the Art Institute of Indiana which offered extensive courses in the culinary Arts. Once Ray dipped her toe in the cooking world, she never looked back.

When Valeria graduated, she worked in French restaurants in the Indianapolis area until she became the head chef at one of the 5-star establishments in the area. Valeria's attention to taste and visual detail caught the eye of a local business person who expressed an interest in publishing her recipes. Valeria began her secondary career authoring cookbooks and e-books which she tackled with as much talent and gusto as her first career. Her passion for food leaps off the page of her books which have colourful anecdotes and stunning pictures of dishes she has prepared herself.

Valeria Ray lives in Indianapolis with her husband of 15 years, Tom, her daughter, Isobel and their loveable Golden Retriever, Goldy. Valeria enjoys cooking special dishes in her large, comfortable kitchen where the family gets involved in preparing meals. This successful, dynamic chef is an inspiration to culinary students and novice cooks everywhere.

•••••••••• • • • • • • •••••••

Author's Afterthoughts

Thank you for Purchasing my book and taking the time to read it from front to back. I am always grateful when a reader chooses my work and I hope you enjoyed it!

With the vast selection available online, I am touched that you chose to be purchasing my work and take valuable time out of your life to read it. My hope is that you feel you made the right decision.

I very much would like to know what you thought of the book. Please take the time to write an honest and informative review on Amazon.com. Your experience and opinions will be of great benefit to me and those readers looking to make an informed choice.

With much thanks,

Valeria Ray

Printed in Great Britain
by Amazon